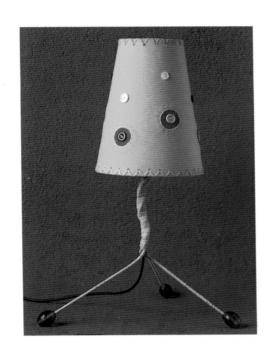

the
colourful home

the colourful home

an inspirational sourcebook of decorative schemes

SALLY WALTON

LORENZ BOOKS

First published by Lorenz Books in 2000

© Anness Publishing Limited 2000

Lorenz Books is an imprint of Anness Publishing Limited

Hermes House, 88-89 Blackfriars Road, London SE1 8HA

Published in the USA by Lorenz Books

Anness Publishing Inc., 27 West 20th Street,

New York, NY 10011; (800) 354-9657

Distributed in Canada by Raincoast Books

8680 Cambie Street, Vancouver

British Columbia V6P 6M9

Publisher Joanna Lorenz
Senior Editor Caroline Davison
Project Editor Emma Hardy
Production Controller Claire Rae
Photographers Rodney Forte, Michelle Garrett, Lizzie
Orme, Steven Pam, Graham Rae,
Adrian Taylor, Peter Williams
Contributors Deena Beverley, Lisa Brown,
Victoria Brown, Sacha Cohen, Diana Civil,
Mary Fellows, Emma Hardy, Paul Jackson,
Alison Jenkins, Mary Maguire, Maggie Philo,
Stewart Walton, Josephine Whitfield
Stylists Lisa Brown, Katie Gibbs, Jo Rigg,
Georgina Rhodes, Leeann Mackenzie, Catherine Tully

10 9 8 7 6 5 4 3 2 1

contents

introduction

This book will help you discover the power of colour and understand how it can be used to create the environment you want. The following chapters are devoted to particular colours, exploring their impact at full intensity and in a range of shades, tints and tones. The colours are shown in real rooms with many different styles of furniture and accessories illuminated by both natural and artificial light.

Colour can be warm or cool, can calm or excite us, can make small rooms look more spacious, or cavernous rooms feel cosy. It can hide a multitude of sins or bring interesting architectural details sharply into focus. It has the potential to elevate and envigorate your interior decorating.

Fashion also has a part to play. A fashionable colour scheme can be exciting and refreshing and bring a dowdy room right up to date. But remember that decorating is very big business nowadays and, to keep sales up, the market demands that those fashions keep changing all the time. It is best to try to remain subjective and not be too swayed by ever-changing trends, because you have to be able to live comfortably with your colour choices.

Trust your feelings, explore the possibilities and enrich your life with a greater understanding of colour.

how colour works

The study of colour in a purely scientific way began with Sir Isaac Newton in 1676. His experiments with light led him to shine pure white light through a glass prism and reflect it onto a neutral-coloured surface. The result was a continuous band of merging colour, ranging from red through orange, yellow, green, blue and violet. The rainbow is nature's version of Newton's experiment. Light passing through drops of rain projects the spectrum colours across the sky.

The Colour Wheel

To explain colour, scientists constructed the colour wheel, which separated the spectrum into twelve different colours. This was done by first drawing a triangle divided into three equal sections for the primary colours – red, yellow and blue. These are called primary because they cannot be mixed from a combination of any other colours. They, along with black and white, form the basis of all other colours.

The primary colours are placed in an equilateral triangle with yellow at the top, red lower right and blue lower left. A compass is used to draw the wheel around it and then divide it into twelve equal sections. The primary colours then fill the sections opposite their position in the triangle.

Secondary colours – orange, green and violet – are made by mixing equal parts of two of the primaries: yellow and red make orange, yellow and blue make green, blue and red make violet. These colours fill the spaces midway between each of the two primaries.

Tertiary colours are made by mixing a secondary colour with an equal amount of the colour next to it on the wheel: yellow and orange make golden-yellow, red and orange make burnt orange, yellow and green make lime green, blue and green make turquoise, blue and violet make indigo, red and violet make crimson. Arranging colours in this way helps us to see the effects that can be achieved when they are used alongside and opposite each other.

Colour Theory

It is worth taking time to understand something of colour theory because our perception of colour is mainly a physiological phenomenon. Our eyes encounter different colours as wavelengths of light, and our brain recognizes

Using a colour wheel
helps us to understand
the theory of colour,
allowing us to use
colour effectively in
the home.

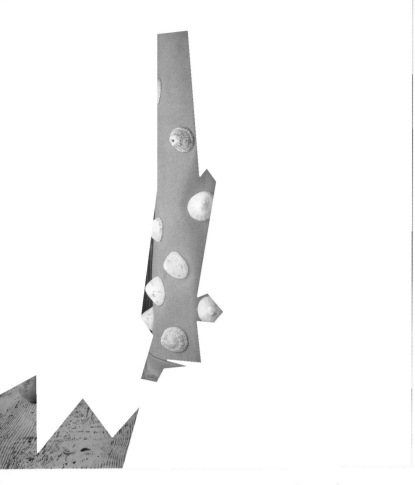

ABOVE **The soft fabric of this orange lamp gives a subtly coloured glow.**

OPPOSITE **These contrasting lamps in shades of red and yellow provide a warm light and are guaranteed to brighten up your room.**

The existence of colour depends entirely upon light. This can be demonstrated by placing a red vase on a table in a room directly lit by a standard tungsten bulb. Turn off the light and the vase is no longer red, but black like everything else in the dark room. The colour of any object is only a visual experience and not an actual fact!

This has all to do with the power of a surface to absorb or reflect light particles. Red appears to be red because it absorbs all the other colours of the spectrum and reflects only the red. Illuminate it with a green light and it will no longer be red but black. It may just be a trick of the light, but that, in essence, is what colour is.

You may wonder how important this is to interior decorating, and the answer is probably not very, but colour is a powerful tool and the more you know, the more chance you have of using its properties to the maximum. So stay with it.

A hue is one of the pure colours of the spectrum, such as red or yellow, and it can be used to describe other colours. For example lavender has a violet hue, olive has a green hue, or pink has a red hue.

Colours opposite each other on the colour wheel are called complementary. These are colours of equal intensity. When they are combined in equal proportions they make a neutral grey. Alongside each other they are at their most intense. If you concentrate your eyes on a single colour for a few seconds then shut them or stare at a white or neutral grey, you will

and interprets this information. Red, as the colour of danger, is not a random choice: it is transmitted on the highest frequency and is recognized faster than any of the other colours. As a warning, it is immediate. Red advances, appearing closer, while blue recedes. A room in which the walls are painted red will appear smaller than one with walls that are painted blue.

find the complementary of the colour you were looking at appears before you. This is known as after image. The eye produces this contrast to achieve a state of equilibrium, returning once more to what is most comfortable and balanced. Artists who study colour theory will sometimes exploit this effect to create discomfort and to arouse emotion in the viewer. When decorating it helps to know the relative power of the different colour combinations, if only so you know which ones to avoid.

Colour contrasts occur on several levels. The simplest to understand is a contrast of hue, which describes the difference between undiluted colours seen alongside each other. Yellow/red/blue, being the primaries, represent the most extreme example of this. There are also hot/cold contrasts – the red, yellow, orange side being hot, and the blue, green, violet side being cold. The most extreme hot/cold contrasts that exist are red-orange and blue-green.

A scientific experiment was conducted involving the same group of people spending time at the same level of activity in the same workroom, which was first painted in cold colours and then in warm colours. The actual room temperature was very gradually lowered and the level at which they first felt cold was 11C°/52°F degrees in the red-orange room and 15C°/59°F degrees in the blue-green room.

It was concluded that colour has the power to increase or decrease the circulation. So it really does make sense to paint a cold room in warm colours.

Another type of colour contrast is light and dark. This contrast is very clear if you look at both a colour and a black-and-white version of the same photograph. Red and green have the same tonal quality and show up as an equal grey on the black-and-white version. Yellow and violet are the most extreme examples of light/dark contrast apart from black and white, which are not colours but tones.

OPPOSITE **The varying shades of blue in this table setting complement each other perfectly.**

ABOVE RIGHT **Create a striking colour contrast with this pink and blue cushion.**

RIGHT **The crisp texture of this cerise lamp makes a bold statement against the blue background.**

The addition of white to a colour produces a tint, which we call a pastel colour; black darkens a colour to produce a tone.

A harmony is a combination of colours that allows the eye to travel smoothly between them. Colours that are close to each other on the colour wheel will harmonize: orange, yellow and red, for example. Colours that do not naturally harmonize, such as orange and crimson, can be made to do so by the addition of white. On a standard paint colour chart most colours are highly diluted with white because most people find choosing colour a difficult commitment to make.

Personal Taste

Quite apart from the science of colour, there is a subjective element to colour choice. People do favour certain colours, and no amount of theory will persuade someone to paint a room a vivid shade of yellow or red if they are of a calmer blue-grey disposition.

Fortunately we are all individuals and personal taste varies enormously, but it is still essential to recognize that these basic colour laws exist and to have a good understanding of how colour works. At least then, when you break those rules in a surge of creativity, you will be aware of what it is you are doing.

OPPOSITE **A green curtain with a bright red lining provides a striking contrast.**

RIGHT **The chalky blue of the walls perfectly complements the red curtain.**

yellow

The colour of the sun carries within it the power to compensate for a lack of natural sunlight, which makes it indispensable if you are decorating in a dull, grey climate.

Yellow expands, warms and brightens north-facing rooms. Walls that have been painted yellow give off a glow of light, like an aura, which advances to influence the atmosphere of the whole room. Tonally, yellow is the lightest colour in the spectrum, and it is associated with positive moods. Warm, mellow yellows come from natural earth pigments and harmonize well with reds, browns and oranges, whereas the sharp, cool yellows, such as lemon and chrome yellow, are derived from chemicals and look best alongside other cool colours, such as light blue, pale grey and lavender.

"naturally bright buttercups and daffodils
to the metallic brightness of brass and gold"

yellow palette

The expression "yellow palette" is used to describe those colours in which yellow is the dominant hue. They range from naturally bright buttercups and daffodils to the metallic brightness of brass and gold, and from the palest Jersey cream to vibrant and sharp lemon curd. Those yellows from the red side of the colour wheel will harmonize in all their tints and tones, as will those on the green side. Balance a predominantly yellow colour scheme by adding small touches of its complementaries, blue or purple, and your eyes will rest easy.

BELOW A background of Primrose Yellow gives a strong, modern look.

BELOW Lemon Zest and lime green create an intense citric harmony.

BELOW Sunshine Yellow roses are punctuated with green foliage.

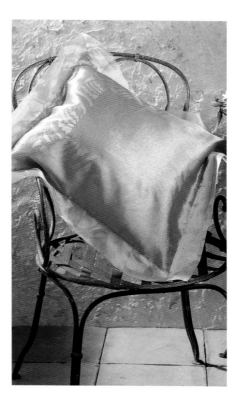

ABOVE **The Gold in these gilded bay leaves has a cool sheen.**

ABOVE **Orange Sorbet brings a warm welcome to a cold steel chair.**

ABOVE **Tangerine Dream gives a sophisticated look.**

BELOW **Cinnamon Spice adds a subtle warmth to walls.**

BELOW **Cappuccino Coffee gives a naturally elegant finish.**

BELOW **Cocoa Brown provides a meltingly rich backdrop.**

This is a refreshing colour, and its name instantly evokes images of clumps of pale primroses growing on grassy banks in early spring. The colour is like the flower after which it is named: cool and self-illuminating, but with the ability to gather strength and thrive when bathed in warm light.

Primrose appears on the blue-green side of yellow on the colour wheel. Although naturally cool, it carries a promise of warmth, which can be best brought out if it is used in combination with its complementary, a reddish-purple.

primrose yellow

Nature does not make mistakes with its colour associations, and primrose yellow, pale and tinged with green, provides the relaxing element in a woodland stroll when it is combined with light moss green and deep violet. Use it with white, pale grey and black for a sharper urban look – this is the perfect colour scheme for an airy loft conversion.

ABOVE **Yellow flowers add another dimension to this colour scheme. The effect is intense but harmonious, because all these colours have a yellow hue.**

LEFT **The red chilli (chile) flowerheads perfectly complement the primrose yellow and inject an up-to-the-minute note of heat in an elegantly stylish setting.**

string bottles

Colour alters according to the texture of the surface. These three bottles have been wrapped in string, which matches the colour of the smooth paintwork around them, but their texture makes them stand out. Choose bottles with interesting shapes, and turn them into works of art.

You Will Need
ball of string
glue gun with all-purpose glue sticks
3 interestingly shaped bottles
scissors

1 Coil one end of the string round like a drinks mat. Heat the glue gun, then apply glue in spokes over the base. Press the string on to them. To make the base secure, draw a ring of glue around the edge.

2 Circle the bottle with the string, working your way up and applying glue as you go. Make sure you get a good bonding on the bends. When you reach the top of the bottle, cut the end of the string and apply glue to prevent fraying. Repeat these steps with the other bottles.

RIGHT Black, white and lemon, combined with the unfussy, straight lines of the stained glass, add an art deco feel. The brave choice of bright lemon for the walls was inspired by the small segments of the colour in the door panels. It works, and the overall effect is stunning.

OPPOSITE The lemon yellow wall lights up the natural light browns of the cane, wood and string in this arrangement.

BELOW AND BELOW RIGHT A clean colour for the kitchen, lemon yellow can be warmed with liberal sprinklings of dark red. Restrict the incidence of other colours and allow the yellow to dominate.

energizing
colours full of
lemon zest

lemon zest

Lemon yellow is such a distinctive colour
and so inseparably linked to the fruit that the sight of it can
bring the sharp, tangy taste to the mouth. The coolest of
the yellows, it has brilliance but no warmth, which gives
it a sophistication that the sunnier golden-yellows lack.
 The colour was impossible to mix from an earth
pigment and was introduced to the artist's and
decorator's palette in the late 18th century
when chrome yellow, a lead-based pigment, was first
manufactured. It immediately became the height of
fashion for elegant interiors during the late Georgian
and Regency periods. The sombre Victorians
did not like it much, but it was used
widely in the 1920s before coming
back to the forefront of fashion in
the 1950s.

Yellow Jewel Chair

Transform an old armchair into a desirable object with simple upholstery. Stretchy fabrics make it easier to achieve a professional finish, but any upholstery fabric is suitable.

1 Remove all old covers from the armchair. Sand the varnish from the frame. Seal with a clear wax or silicone polish. Use the old covers as a template and cut the fabric to size, with a generous allowance for the back rest.

3 Cut the fabric to fit the back surface of the back rest and apply rubber adhesive to the fabric and chair. When tacky, apply the fabric, covering the staples and the turned-over edges. Hammer a tack into each corner.

2 Stretch the fabric over the back rest until it is hand-tight and staple it in place. Secure, in order, the top, bottom and sides with one or two staples in the centre, before applying lines of staples to keep the fabric taut.

4 Trace the cushion shape on to the card. Cut out and staple to the cushion. Wrap the fabric around the cushion and staple to the card. Attach a layer of fabric to the underside of the cushion using rubber adhesive.

sunshine yellow

Golden sunshine yellow exudes ripeness, warmth and
happiness. Its intensity and brilliance can, literally, light up a room that
has limited natural light. It can also be overpowering unless the eye is
allowed some respite in the form of its complementary colour. Small
splashes of cobalt blue and some white will balance the effect without
dulling the yellow. When it is used in combination with its true
complementary, purple, the contrast is quite visually disturbing.

Imagine a field of sunflowers against an azure sky and you will be
seeing sunshine yellow at its best. Seen up close, the sunflower offers us
another good guide to which colours combine successfully with sunshine
yellow. Natural earth colours tinged with red, such as terracotta, red
ochre and burnt sienna, will harmonize well, while deep brown or black
will give the most dramatic light–dark contrast.

ABOVE The sunflowers,
with their large, brown
seed-heads, dominate this
group of yellow flowers.
Unassuming containers
make certain that the
flowers are the centre
of attention.

OPPOSITE The terracotta
wall colour provides a
strong, harmonious
background for the vibrant
sunshine yellow chair. The
flowers enhance the effect
by carrying the yellow over
into the arrangement and
keeping the other blooms
within the yellow palette.

frieze frames

You Will Need
lining paper
ruler
craft knife
yellow emulsion
(latex) paint
PVA glue
medium paintbrushes
small, sharp scissors
green paper
yellow ochre acrylic
paint`

Print-rooms were all the rage in the late 18th and early 19th centuries. Black-and-white prints of Greek and Roman temples and classical views were cut out and pasted directly on to walls in formal framed arrangements, and this pale yellow was the standard background colour. This project shows how to create an elegant print-room frieze with a touch of colour.

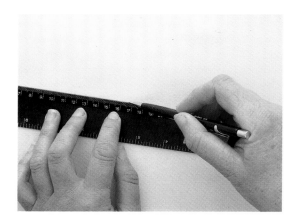

1 Measure the lining paper to the required length and depth of your frieze. Cut along the edge using a ruler and craft knife. Mix three parts yellow emulsion paint with one part PVA. Add a little water to allow the mixture to flow more easily. Use this to paint the lining paper.

2 Choose a motif and take as many photocopies as necessary to cover the length of the border. Cut them out with scissors. Cut the green paper into equal short lengths. Tear along the top edge to represent greenery.

3 Arrange and glue down the buildings and torn paper along the length of the frieze.

4 Glue down the swag motifs along the top edge of the frieze.

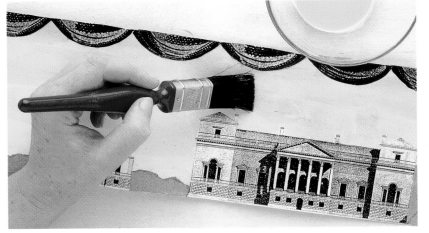

5 Mix a little yellow ochre acrylic paint into some PVA glue. Then dilute four parts tinted glue with one part water. Brush the tinted, diluted glue over the frieze to seal and protect it.

shell frames

You Will Need
wooden frame
gold spray paint
shells
scrap paper
strong glue
china marker

Gold highlights a good shape and exaggerates a bad one. The perfect symmetry of these scallop shells is naturally decorative and too fine a gift to be left behind on the beach. Take a few home in your pocket and use them to make this stylishly simple golden frame.

1 In a well-ventilated area, cover your work surface with scrap paper and spray the wooden frame with the gold paint. Let dry.

2 Place the shells on some scrap paper, ensuring they are welll spaced. Spray them evenly with the gold paint. Let dry.

3 Arrange and glue the shells to the frame with strong glue. Mark their positions first with a china marker as each shell is different.

gold

Gold, the yellow metal, has been a symbol of wealth since the beginning of civilization, and because its supply is limited, it has always been highly valued. Until recently gold would not have been used to decorate a home unless it was a palace or a bordello. These days all that glitters is definitely not gold, and you can buy very convincing water-based gold paint in a range of shades suitable for walls and furniture.

TOP Fill gilded seashells with wax to make gleaming candles.

ABOVE Gold can add lustre to special occasions.

LEFT This lovely bentwood chair has been gilded with an application of gold leaf on a white background to give a pale gold effect.

orange sorbet

This orange has a light, juicy quality, which is diluted in intensity but not dulled by the addition of white. It is the colour of orange ice lollies (popsicles), goldfish, red lentils, ripe nectarines and sun-bleached life jackets. It carries warmth that does not overpower in the way that a brighter or deeper shade of orange would. It is a good choice of wall colour for a child's north-facing playroom, especially if the natural sunlight is weak and indirect. It is also a good colour for kitchens and dining rooms, but it is not relaxing and is perhaps best avoided in bedrooms or sitting rooms. Accents of cool blue-grey or sage green are naturally complementary, and a metallic silver grey will give it an up-to-the-moment look.

shades of **orange sorbet** burst with irresistible warmth

LEFT The muted orange works particularly well with its complementary colour, blue.

ABOVE Sheer curtains give an impression of warmth.

OPPOSITE Natural wood and silver work well with these orange napkins.

tangerine dream

Tangerine is a sassy, youthful colour, a flamboyant younger cousin to orange. It is full of life and can be used to inject freshness and sparkle. Balance it with flashes of ice blue or pale jade green, but create paths of light cream or off-white between them.

This is a great colour to use in a small bathroom with white fixtures. It looks good alongside chrome, aluminium and bare wood. Use it on a single wall in a contemporary home surrounded by pale, neutral shades, or in an entrance hall, where its welcoming energy will be put to good use. An orange environment is also said to improve social behaviour and make people feel less hostile.

ABOVE Take your inspiration from nature's perfection with Chinese lantern pods to reinforce an orange theme.

OPPOSITE Tangerine looks vibrant alongside its next-door neighbours on the spectrum, red and yellow. White adds light, and a dark pewter grey gives a dramatic contrast.

shades of orange

Orange is one of nature's indicators, showing us that fruit is ripe, that summer has ended and that autumn has arrived. When the sun is low in the sky its light is more gentle than in summer and we can see the true beauty of the colour. Take this idea into the home, using subtle washes of light rather than a bright central light pendant for an orange room.

Team it with natural materials such as raffia, hessian (burlap) and wood to give a minimalist room real warmth. Alternatively, sharpen the orange with silver, as with the starbursts below, to give a wall an expensive-looking wallpaper treatment on a budget. A harmonious mood can be created by using fruit and flowers to carry the same colour forwards into the room.

cinnamon spice

The spice's powdery texture and distinctive smell are inseparable from the colour itself. Try conjuring up a picture of cinnamon swirled through golden-yellow pastry: it is warm, comforting and utterly delicious.

The colour works well when it is applied as a wash rather than as flat colour, and it is best used within the context of its natural associations and origins. This is the colour of baked mud walls, clay pots, worn, polished wood and tanned suede. To show off its richness use it with bitter chocolate and pale cream, accented with small splashes of golden-yellow.

THIS PAGE Natural fabrics in warm cinnamon colours are woven loosely together to create this rustic blind.

OPPOSITE TOP LEFT Brilliant primary colours work well against rusty spice walls.

OPPOSITE TOP RIGHT A pale yellow ochre and cinnamon wash combined with bands of pale green creates the Tuscan villa look.

OPPOSITE BELOW LEFT Natural materials are used in a calm, stylish work space.

OPPOSITE BELOW RIGHT The spice brown colours of oiled and polished wood are rich and varied.

warm, **comforting** and utterly **delicious**

cappuccino brown

The mixture of coffee and cream creates a unique shade of brown with a smart urban edge. Browns like this, together with cream shag-pile carpets and supple suede upholstery, have enjoyed a recent fashion revival. Simplicity is the key to success. Keep the walls white, use dark-stained natural wood for shelves and glass, leather and chrome for furniture, and hang plain blinds at the windows. Cushions and throws in sensuous fabrics – silk, and chenille, for example – can be used to add softening touches, but do limit your choice to shades of brown.

soothing tones of **mocha**
toffee and **walnut**

OPPOSITE **Coffee-coloured walls look good in a modern setting, but good lighting is essential because the colour radiates very little light of its own.**

LEFT **Natural wood floor slats in shades of cappuccino are inset** with broad blocks of pale cream to create a dramatic floor pattern.

BELOW A simple hopsack cloth set with white porcelain reveals how a limited palette can give striking results.

sensuous shades of the richest **chocolate brown**

LEFT A chocolate ponyskin pattern can be easily stencilled on to a lampshade to give it a Wild West look.

BELOW The real thing – a chocolate and cream sundae.

OPPOSITE An intricately carved wooden screen; the patterned fabric and clay pots re-create a North African look.

cocoa brown

Whether you prefer melt-in-the-mouth milk chocolate or the snappy bitterness of dark chocolate, few of us need to be reminded of its colour. This is the richest of the browns, veering toward red and black in its dark tones and pale mushroom brown when it is diluted with white.

Although it is seldom used as a wall colour, it comes into its own when it is used with discretion with white or a pale earth colour. At its darkest it can be comfortably surrounded by almost any colour in any degree of brilliance; when it is lighter it is best used with harmonious earthy shades. Chocolate brown and ivory white was a popular combination in American colonial-style interiors.

red

The most prominent of all colours, red demands and receives our attention. One of the three primary colours, whose complementary is green, it ranges through hot orange-red to cool red-violet. Red has both positive and negative associations. In some cultures it is the colour of love and life, in others it represents danger. Decorating with red is considered brave, bold and challenging. In the past red was derived from crushed beetles, baked-earth pigments, and roots and minerals. These days we can choose any shade of red and have it copied synthetically, so we are free to re-create the colour of Georgian dining rooms, Gothic stained glass, 1950s polka dots or faded Tuscan frescoes.

"decorating with red is brave,
bold and challenging"

red palette

When the earthy rust colours produce warm, friendly and relaxed feelings, the red palette is rich and welcoming, but at the other extreme, where we find purple, steeped in ceremony and magic, it is inclined to make us feel uneasy and anxious. Mix white with any red to dissipate these sensory challenges and create a pastel pink or lavender.

Solid red can be too dominating if it is used over large areas, but it will provide uplift when used as part of a pattern or in splashes as drapes, throws, cushions or floral arrangements.

BELOW **Poppy Red is a dramatic colour choice.**

BELOW **Crimson and mauve is a lively combination.**

BELOW **Rusty Red is a deep, rich, warm colour.**

ABOVE **Raspberry Pink against white** walls creates maximum impact.

ABOVE **Shocking Pink gives walls** a modern feel.

ABOVE **Pastel Pink carries** positive connotations.

BELOW **Strawberry Cream is rich,** ripe and simply delicious.

BELOW **Vivid Violet is deep, rich** and cool.

BELOW **Purple Passion can be tamed** with a vibrant aqua blue.

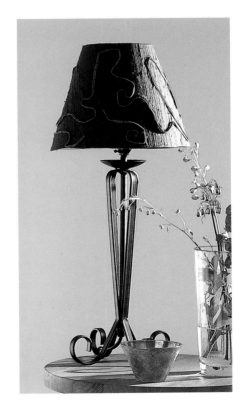

poppy red

Anyone who has seen a yellow cornfield streaked with bright red poppies on a sunny day will know what an unbeatable combination red, straw yellow and sky blue make. Poppy red is associated with bravery and bravado in decorating: you have to feel courageous to choose this colour for your walls, so be prepared to defend your choice! Because red advances visually, it will make a room look smaller if it is used on all four walls, but the effect can be used to advantage in a long, thin room to pull the opposite walls towards each other.

Poppy red works best alongside its neighbours on the yellow side of the colour wheel, because they take their share of its impact. However, it sets up an intense energy field when it is used alongside crimson and violet. For a metallic contrast choose a rich antique gold.

The combination of the bright golden-yellow lampshade and poppy red wall glows like a roaring fire.

cornfields **streaked** with **bright** red poppies

poppy flowers

Poppies are all the more precious because the flowers do not last long when they have been cut. Luckily, the texture of the petals resembles paper and the simple shapes are easily copied to make very convincing fakes. Use the brightest red paper for the petals.

You Will Need
garden wire
cotton wool
(surgical cotton)
yellow, black, red
and green crêpe paper
sticky tape
scissors
glue

1 To make the stem, cut a length of garden wire. Bend the top to make a loop and trap a small amount of cotton wool (surgical cotton) in the loop. Cover this in a cut-out circle of yellow crêpe paper. Secure by wrapping tape around it.

2 Cut out three small circles of black crêpe paper and fringe the outer edges. Push the end of the wire through the centres. Cut out five petal shapes in red crêpe paper and stretch the outer edges until they frill. Glue the petals, around the centre of the base.

3 Finally, cover the stem in green crêpe paper by winding a long strip diagonally around and securing it at the base with sticky tape.

49

crimson skies

The colour crimson is a red tinged with blue. It originated as cochineal, a dye made from the dried bodies of insects, which were gathered from cacti in Mexico. Its brilliance and rarity made it a very expensive colour, and its use implied great wealth.

In countries such as India and Mexico, crimson is used in potent combinations with ultramarine blue, banana yellow, lime green and dazzling white.

In the softer light of more temperate climates, it imparts a wonderful warmth and sexiness when it is combined with silvery sage green or shades of violet.

crimson, rust and golden-yellow

OPPOSITE Although the furniture is of Eastern origin, it is ultimately the colour that transports us into an exotic dreamworld. The use of semi-sheer fabric for the drapes means that only the minimum of hand-stitching is needed.

LEFT The brilliant combination of crimson, rust and golden-yellow glows with intensity. This shows us how a sense of mood and place can be established simply through the use of colour.

BELOW Candlelight suits the colour crimson well, as is evident in this rosy winter arrangement.

pleated tissue blind

You Will Need
wallpaper paste
pasting brush
hand-made tissue
paper
tape measure
scissors
double-sided tape
ruler
pencil
eyelet tool and
eyelets
2 small tassels
to match thin,
coloured cord
staple gun
wooden batten to fit
window recess
2 screw eyes

Delicate hand-made tissue paper makes a surprisingly sturdy blind. To give extra depth to the colour, we pasted two sheets of the crimson paper together. When the light shines through, it vibrates with colour.

1 Mix up the wallpaper paste following the manufacturer's instructions and paste together two sheets of tissue paper. Leave to dry. Measure the window recess, adding 5cm/2in to the width and 15cm/6in to the length. Cut to size and apply the double-sided tape to the sides.

3 On the back of the blind, mark horizontal lines with a ruler and pencil 5cm/2in apart. Fold the blind into regular pleats along the marked lines. Use an eyelet tool to pierce holes on both seams, at the centre of each pleat. Insert the eyelets.

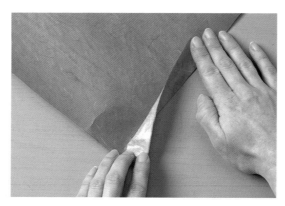

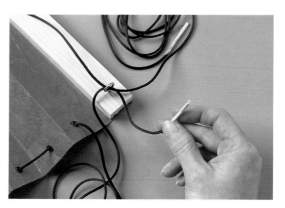

2 Remove the backing paper and fold a 2.5cm/1in hem down each side. Apply double-sided tape to the lower edge of the blind then fold a 2.5cm/1in hem along its length.

4 Tie a tassel to the end of a length of cord and pass it through the eyelets. Repeat on the other side. With the staple gun attach the blind to the top of the wooden batten and place the screw eyes at each end. Thread through the cord so that the two ends hang to one side of the blind.

rusty red

Whether it is called terracotta, red ochre, Indian red, rust, brick red, ox blood or barn red, this colour has a universal appeal, and we all recognize its familiar warmth. The variety of shades, from bright rust through to deep red-brown, can be safely mixed together, and because it is the colour of earth, wood and leather, there are few colours with which it cannot be happily combined. Deep purple, sea green and dark grey are popular choices, and they will look sensational with a pale neutral between them.

Rusty red looks sharp and smart when it is combined with black and cream, but, for a dreamy effect, try pale ice blue, and greens and reds will produce a more rustic result. Use it matt and chalky as a colour wash on walls to give an ethnic look, or as a flat oil colour on skirtings (baseboards) and floorboards.

ABOVE LEFT **These two shades of rust red create a rich backdrop for a display of dried roses.**

LEFT **Elaborate mirror mouldings and elegant soft furnishings contrast with the roughest of paint treatments to create a deliberate look of "faded splendour".**

OPPOSITE **The lampshade is made from sheets of undyed bark. As the light shines through, the effect is stunning.**

napkin rings

You Will Need
fine galvanized wire
ruler or tape measure
wire cutters
round-nosed
jewellery pliers
plastic bottle to use
as former
glass rocaille beads
in pink and red
fine silver wire

This is a brilliant project for a rainy day and will bring instant sunshine to the dinner table. The tiny glass beads in shades of pink and red catch and reflect the light, contrasting perfectly with crisp, white napkins. Wired rocaille beads, woven into simple designs, shimmer in the candlelight and make delicate yet sumptuous ornaments for the dinner table.

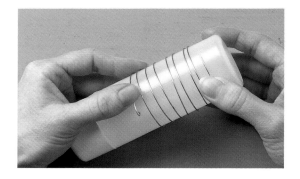

1 Take about 2m/2yd of galvanized wire and bend a small loop in one end. Wind the wire about ten times around the plastic bottle.

2 Thread enough pink glass beads on to the wire to fit around the bottle once, then change to red and thread another round of beads. Repeat until the wire is full, then bend a loop with pliers.

3 Bend the beaded wire around the bottle to restore its shape. Secure a length of fine silver wire to the first row, then bind it around the others. Do this at two or three other points around the napkin ring. When the ring is complete, wind the ends of the silver wires back around the previous rows to neaten, and snip off the excess.

raspberry ripple

A youthful and exuberant red

that manages to be both energetic and cool, raspberry red's complementary colour is pistachio green, and they are an unbeatable summer-invoking combination. Until recently, only the brave dared use raspberry red as a solid wall colour, but it often appeared in floral patterns. The rosebud wallpapers and fabrics popular in the 1950s have come right back into fashion, but now we have both the paint colours and the courage to match them. On its own, raspberry red can have a cold, rather impersonal feel, but it is very responsive to other colours. For a brilliant Rajasthani-style colour scheme try raspberry red with burnt orange, turquoise, silver frames, lamps and accessories.

ABOVE RIGHT Rich raspberry red flowers are complemented by a soft, white wrapping and a purple bow.

RIGHT To make this bedroom wall colour, a raspberry colour wash has been applied on top of a base coat of yellow. The result is a patchy, glowing pink, which sits happily alongside the orange-yellow woodwork.

youthful, energetic shades of
raspberry red

shocking pink

The name says it all: a pink so arrestingly bright that it stops you in your tracks. It is an extrovert colour, always attention seeking, and even when white is added it manages to grab the limelight. To re-create a 1950s style, use shocking pink with black or white in polka dots or stripes, and, for a 1960s or 1970s look, go for colour clashes by introducing bright orange, purple or scarlet. If retro is not your style, use the pink alongside rich ethnic-looking textiles with other strong, solid colours, such as emerald green or royal blue.

THIS PAGE Shocking pink gives this room a strong contemporary feel when combined with deep purple curtains.

OPPOSITE This group shows the essence of a colour scheme that weaves like a magical thread through a room to pull furniture, fabrics and accessories together and create the atmosphere you want.

pastel pink

This pink is very, very sweet, so be careful
not to overdo it – too much can be sickly! It is a pale
version of crimson, and, like crimson, it contains a touch
of cool blue, edging it towards mauve, which becomes
most apparent if it is used with shades of violet or
lavender. The rather feminine character of this pink
makes it a favourite for floral chintz fabrics.

To keep it looking fresh, use it with an equal amount
of white or let it share the limelight with pale lemon
yellow or mint green. For a more sophisticated look,
wash it over walls and use a pale, matt grey-green for
the woodwork.

create **sweet delights**
with **ice-cream** colours

OPPOSITE **Create a nostalgic haze with these romantic pink curtains.**

LEFT **The luscious pink combines well with grey-green eucalyptus foliage.**

BELOW **The glass dish in the foreground of this group gives a cooling violet cast to all the shades of pink and white in this table setting, creating a fresh, romantic, floral arrangement.**

pink windows

These pinks are chalky pastels which look good in each other's company, so mix powder blue, pale lemon and pistachio green together for a youthful colour scheme. Look out for new paints based on distemper (tempera), which will match the colour and the texture of real sherbet by drying to a soft chalky bloom. These are the perfect colours for a nursery or a seaside holiday home where the emphasis is strictly on having fun.

strawberry cream

This is the most delicious shade of pink, which is made by mixing small amounts of scarlet with lots of creamy white. As a strawberry ripens, it turns from green to white, then yellow before finally becoming bright and juicy scarlet; when scarlet is used to make pink, the yellow in it re-emerges to warm and soften the colour. The resulting pink is a joy to live with.

It is a favourite colour for the exterior of thatched cottages in Suffolk, England, where it starts out as a bright pink but is soon faded by the sun, wind and rain. In country interiors it can be applied as a colour wash to give a traditional plaster pink, which suits antique furniture and fabrics very well.

OPPOSITE Pink succeeds in bringing a warm atmosphere into a potentially cold, minimalist space.

BELOW Harmonious shades of burgundy, brown and pink contrast with cool green.

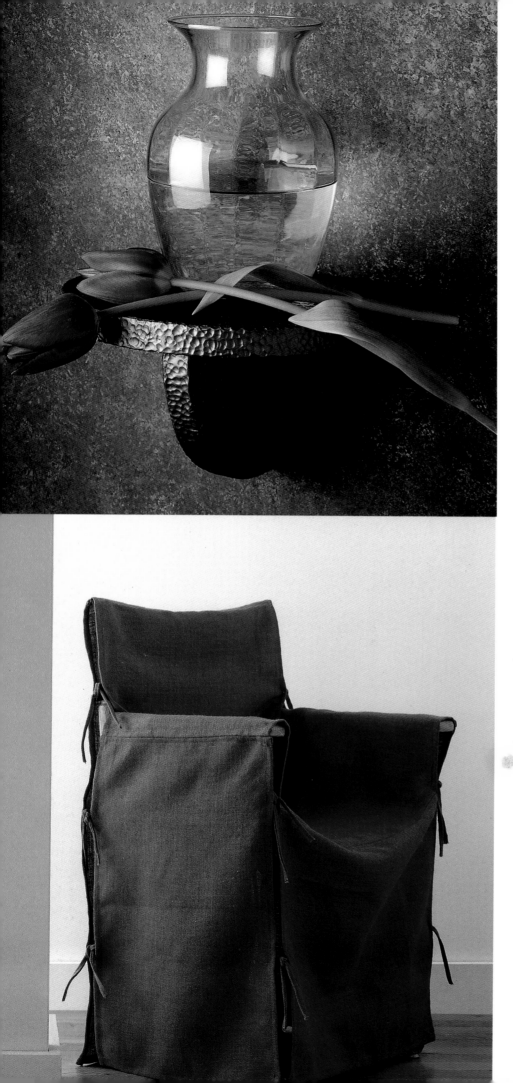

vivid violet

The colour violet absorbs light, and it has depth and intensity. It is, however, completely altered by the proximity of other colours, red making it look more purple, while blue turns it to indigo. At its purest, violet is best used as an accent or part of a pattern rather than as a solid block of wall colour. Diluted with white, it produces lavender shades, which are much easier to live with and look great with other tints, such as warm pink, grey and primrose yellow. Violet's complementary colour is a bright butter yellow, and together these provide the strongest light–dark colour contrast.

ABOVE LEFT **The stark pewter combines well with the richly coloured tulip.**

LEFT **Colours as strong as this look fantastic against plain white walls and polished wooden floors.**

OPPOSITE **Set these beautiful beaded picture frames, in shades of blue, purple and violet, against a vivid background.**

purple passion

Historically, this rich colour has been associated with royalty, high rank and the Christian church. The Romans used rare shellfish to make purple dyes, and the colour was beloved by Victorians. Aniline dyes, invented in the mid-19th century, made purple accessible to all, and it became popular for home furnishings. It did not come back into favour until the purple craze of the 1960s, when it was used in lurid combinations with orange or shocking pink. Adding purple accessories to a room can instantly make it seem more luxurious. Look out for North African textiles, on which purple is used in unexpected combinations, such as rust, orange, red and black. A rug in these shades can be a good starting point for a colour scheme.

ABOVE **This heart-shaped purple cushion gives a romantic touch to an elegant chair.**

OPPOSITE **Rough matt textures give purple an up-to-date edge, while nature provides a wealth of matching blooms.**

star roller blind

matt emulsion (latex)
paints in purple and yellow
acrylic scumble glaze
paint mixing container
medium paintbrush
plain white roller blind
natural sponge
marker pens in black and gold
paper
scissors
13cm/5in square of high density
sponge, such as upholstery
foam (foam rubber)
craft knife and cutting mat
old plate
bradawl
brass screw eye
blind-pull or tassel

Add a colour wash of purple to a plain white blind, then use its complementary colour, golden-yellow, to add the stars. Use a gold pen for the outlines and match it with a gold tassel pull.

1 Mix some purple emulsion (latex) paint with acrylic scumble glaze. Lay the blind on a flat surface. Dip a natural sponge into the paint and wipe the colour over the blind. Allow to dry.

2 Draw the sun-star design freehand on to a piece of paper and cut it out. Carefully trace the shape on to a piece of high density sponge and cut out.

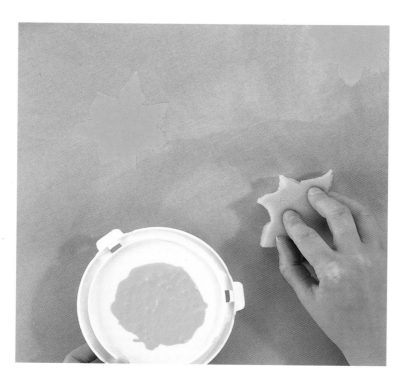

3 Press the sponge into the paint and then on to the blind. Outline each shape and draw in the details using a gold marker pen. Make a hole in the centre of the bottom batten using a bradawl and screw in a small brass eye. Attach a decorative blind-pull or tassel.

blue

Everyone has experienced the clarity of a bright blue sky on a summer's day and the deep, endless blue of the night sky. Blue absorbs light and creates distance. In the landscape blue is the colour of the distant mountains, the sea and the sky – and when we use blue on our walls the space expands. Historically, blue pigments were derived from semi-precious stones, metallic oxides and the plants, indigo and woad. All shades of blue can now be manufactured from chemicals, and the range available for decorators gets wider all the time. The colour is often associated with passive emotions and in the past was thought to have the power to drive away evil.

"the bright sky blue of the Mediterranean appears youthful, rural and full of joy"

blue palette

One of the three primary colours, blue ranges from cool, green-tinged turquoise through to warm, comforting mauve. The colour is often described by the name of the place, which helps to conjure up a particular mood – Mediterranean, Swedish, for example. These blues will also help to create a mood when used in decorating. The bright sky blue of the Mediterranean appears youthful, rural and full of joy, while the pale Swedish grey-blue is calm and reflective. Blue's complementary is orange, and it harmonizes well with green and violet.

BELOW **Navy blue and white makes a classic combination.**

BELOW **Re-create a summer's day with a Royal Blue table setting.**

BELOW **Prussian Blue wood-graining creates an unusual bathroom floor.**

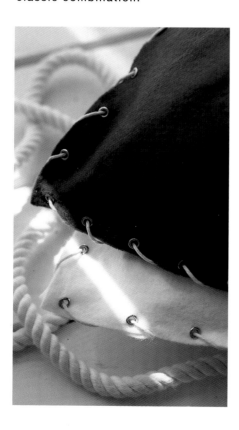

ABOVE Lilac blue fish give a lovely watery effect.

BELOW Sky Blue panelling looks great with fake fur and chrome.

ABOVE Lavender Blue towels are enhanced by a touch of white.

BELOW Aqua Blue glass droplets give a magical, watery feel.

ABOVE A Chalk Blue colour wash makes a perfect backdrop.

BELOW Turquoise accessories are perfect for the bathroom.

navy blue

The colour navy can be so dark that it takes bright daylight to distinguish between it and black, yet it carries none of black's gloomy connotations. Navy blue is crisp, smart, efficient, positive and altogether shipshape.

Navy is seldom seen without its partner, bright white, which our eyes seem to need as reference to confirm that this dark colour is, indeed, a shade of blue. A mixture of ultramarine, cobalt and black, navy blue is available in a wide range of shades, but the colour always retains a pure blue depth that evokes the sky at night.

Navy's complementary colour is yellow-orange, which is why gold blazer buttons always look so striking against the dark fabric.

LEFT Deep navy blue fabric, folded and sewn into textured panels, creates an unusual lampshade.

navy panelling

An inspired way to introduce both colour and texture to an otherwise plain wall is to paint inexpensive timber battens before attaching them to the wall. You'll need to mark the positions of the battens precisely on the wall.

You Will Need

tape measure
wood battens
pencil
saw
paintbrush
emulsion (latex) paint
in 2 colours

spirit level
drill, with masonry and
wood bits
rawl plugs
wood screws

1 Measure the height and width of the wall, to make sure you have equal spacing right up the wall. Cut the wood battens to the required length.

2 Paint the battens on three sides. Use a spirit level to mark the guideline for the first strip. Drill holes in the wall and insert rawl plugs. Drill holes in the wood and then screw the strip in place. Mark the positions for the next wood strip; the space between the strips needs to be absolutely even.

royal blue

Royal blue is a bright, true blue, the familiar colour that appears with red and white on the Union Flag and the primary colour that is so often used alongside yellow and red in children's decorating schemes. Designers of children's toys, books and clothing use this blue because it is the one we recognize first when we learn our colours. It is also the colour of a pattern glaze used on the famous Royal Danish porcelain. It carries positive associations and has a freshening effect when it is introduced in a room as cushions, throws, upholstery or curtains. When it is used next to primaries the effect is harsh and unsophisticated, but it works well in modern settings with its complementary orange, natural wood and a lot of white.

OPPOSITE Fresh blue-and-white gingham ribbon tied in a pretty bow turns a stack of towels into a style statement.

THIS PAGE Blue-and-white patterns can be mixed at will, because the combination of the two will always give a co-ordinated look. Grape hyacinths add a natural touch.

prussian blue

The distinctive dark blue with a violet cast was first manufactured early in the 18th century from a mixture of animal blood burned with alum. Strong blues had previously been very expensive to produce and really only used in paintings, but this new production method was cheaper and the colour became extremely fashionable in house decorating. It has sophistication and looks wonderful alongside straw yellow, dull silver and natural wood. Avoid using it with bright colours, because the contrast will be too strong, and if you want white next to it, choose a white that has been toned down with burnt umber to make it mellower and warmer.

Prussian blues, in a range of light and dark shades, can be found among the historic colour ranges of speciality paint dealers. The colour looks marvellous when used matt on woodwork in a period home or as small areas of bold, dark colour on the walls of a modern room.

OPPOSITE Deep Prussian blues enliven this mosaic but still harmonize with the other blues and shades of green.

BELOW The Prussian blue upholstery and the mosaic, with shades of grey, give a cool, contemporary look.

sophisticated
and elegant **slate** blue

ribbon café curtain

Dress up a small window by making this luxurious striped curtain from ribbons in different shades of blue instead of ordinary fabric. Rows of shiny blue and green glass beads add extra sparkle to the satin, and the larger beads make a pretty hem and add weight so that the ribbons hang evenly.

1 Cut the ribbons to the finished length of the curtain plus 4cm/1½in . Trim one end of each ribbon length into a decorative point.

3 Fold over 5mm/¼in then another 2.5cm/1in along the top edge to make a casing, and tack. Handstitch small glass beads along each seam.

2 Lay out the ribbons in a repeating pattern, alternating satin and chiffon, to fit the width of the window. With a matching thread and a small zigzag stitch, join the ribbons together. End each seam 7.5cm/3in from the bottom.

4 Thread a large plastic bead on to the end of each satin ribbon. Machine-stitch the casing and thread the tension rod or curtain wire through it to hang the curtain.

lilac

Lilac, a warm blue with a rosy cast, is restful to the eye. The colour's name comes from the flowers of the lilac tree, and this is the image it conjures up. One superstition associated with the lilac is that the flowers will bring bad luck if they are brought into the house, but the blooms are so lovely that the tradition is often overlooked. Follow nature's example and use the colours together for a fresh summer look. Lilac can be used to create a tranquil mood with a limited palette of tonally similar shades of pale grey, pink and brown.

warm **lilac** creates
a **tranquil** mood

OPPOSITE Fluffy lilac towels, lotions and
lace arranged for bathtime meditation.

LEFT A stunning arrangement of deep lilac-
coloured hyacinths.

ABOVE Mosaic tiles in tones of lilac and
deeper blues are enhanced by stones.

lilac dreams

White walls are given the palest of pale lilac colour washes before broad stripes are applied in a transparent lilac glaze to give the impression of a wall covered with voile. The border of triangles below the picture rail is easily added using a cardboard template and masking tape. A similar but more natural effect can be created by giving wooden walls a lilac colour wash.

lavender

Lavender blue is a calm, meditative colour, which brings a tranquil atmosphere. The sight of a field of lavender in full bloom against a bright blue sky on a sunny day is not to be missed and is completely unforgettable. This blue prefers the company of its neighbours, blue and green, to its complementary yellow. Sage green, cream, dull silver and sky blue will enhance its calming properties.

THIS PAGE Lavender, cream and black create a serene but sophisitcated look in a living room.

OPPOSITE Heart-shaped lavender bags, tied to an elegant chair, capture a romantic mood.

embossed frame

Tin is a soft metal that can be easily decorated, using a centre punch or a blunt chisel to create dots and lines. Keep your punched design simple and graphic because too much fine detail will get lost when the design is finally punched out.

You Will Need
wooden frame
cardboard
felt-tipped pen
scissors
tape
sheet of tin
centre punch
hammer
tin snips
protective gloves (optional)
chisel
ridged paint scraper
copper nails

1 Lay the wooden frame on a piece of cardboard and draw around the outline with a felt-tipped pen. Add extra length to the outside edges and around the centre to allow for turnings. Cut out the template with scissors. Tape the cardboard template on to a sheet of tin. Mark the corners using a centre punch and hammer, and mark the straight lines with a felt-tipped pen.

3 Lay the wooden frame on the tin and use a ridged paint scraper to coax the metal up the sides of the frame. Turn the frame over and push down the metal edges in the centre, again using the ridged scraper. Cut both strips of tin, each 20 x 2cm/8 x ¼in Snip at the halfway mark and fold at a 90° angle.

2 Cut out the tin shape with tin snips (wear protective gloves to protect your hands from the sharp edges of the tin). Using a hammer and chisel, cut through the centre of the frame in a diagonal line then use the tin snips to cut out the remaining sides and open it out into a square.

4 Nail the strips to the inner edge of the frame, using copper nails. Hammer nails along the outer edges for the frame. Draw a freehand feather design on the tin frame. Use a blunt chisel and hammer to press the design on to the tin in straight lines. Clean the tin with polish and a soft cloth.

chalk blue

Chalk blue is a matt pastel colour, made by softening any shade of bright blue by the addition of white. These blues feel warm and welcoming, and they are the ideal way to give a bedroom or bathroom a feminine look without resorting to a clichéd colour such as pink. The colour's character is enhanced when it is used with a matt finish, and the very best results are achieved with distemper (tempera) paint, which dries to a powdery bloom that intensifies the chalky nature of the colours. As colours mixed with white are more compatible, you won't go wrong if you limit your colour scheme to other pastels.

warm and **welcoming chalk** blues

OPPOSITE Woodwork of mellow cream is the perfect contrast to rich chalk blue.

LEFT Restricting the colour scheme to chalk blue and white gives the room a calm, harmonious atmosphere.

BELOW Deep chalk blue has been used with cream and gold, with an accent of deep purple anemones, to create a sophisticated effect.

sky blue

To describe a colour as sky blue is to look on the bright
side, for this is the blue of the sky on an early summer's morning, holding
the promise of fine, warm weather and good times to come. The same
optimism we feel when we throw open the shutters and see a clear sky is
conveyed when we decorate with this colour. It is also the blue
associated with baby boys, forget-me-nots and faded denim jeans.

Sky blue is hardly ever out of place. In bright or dull company it will
retain its clarity, so feel free to use it with primaries, pastels or neutrals.

ABOVE These walls have
the look of a summer
afternoon sky streaked
with vapour trails.

OPPOSITE Distressed sky
blue shutters are given a
lavender cast by the
proximity of these
fantasy flowers.

aqua blue

Aqua means water, and the colour's name describes a wide range of watery blue-greens. The colour has a restful, calm character, which is best projected when it is used in a combination of harmonious tints and tones. Like water, it can reflect light, a quality much prized in countries in the far northern hemisphere. It can often be seen in elegant Swedish interiors alongside off-white, with highlights of pale gold and against natural bleached pine floors.

THIS PAGE **Create a nautical feel with shades of aqua blue combined with crisp, white cotton.**

restful calming
colours of the sea

LEFT The pale aqua walls of the bathroom are a subtle, sophisticated backdrop for the plaster mirror frame and star motifs.

BELOW Aqua has been used as a pale wash on the walls and as a darker, translucent wood stain on the floor. The horse motif was stamped on to white wood stain.

The colour takes its name from the opaque semi-precious stone associated with the Navajo people of North America, who make exquisite jewellery from the stone and silver. This is the blue-green of Egyptian murals and tropical seas, a light colour in tone and mood, most often used in bathrooms, but equally effective in a garden room that gets a lot of natural sunlight.

Turquoise is a sunny colour, which can take strong contrasts, such as burnt orange, shocking pink or brick red, but control the impact by using plenty of white between them.

turquoise

To keep turquoise cool, use it with a range of blues and greens and the effect will be restful on the eyes.

Egyptian murals and **tropical** seas

ABOVE LEFT **Brilliant shocking pink flowers present the liveliest contrast with the turquoise-coloured vase, and other shades of the colour appear in the patterned table.**

BELOW LEFT **Turquoise and silver baubles cleverly create a link between the cushion cover and the shades of blue on the wall and curtain.**

decorated frame

Wood-graining is quite easy to do and the effect is startlingly realistic when you use the right tool. Two shades of turquoise have been used to change an ordinary window frame into something eye-catching.

You Will Need
sandpaper
pale blue-green
vinyl silk paint
decorator's
paintbrush
deep blue-green matt
emulsion (flat latex)
paint
water-based scumble
heart grainer (rocker)
gloss acrylic varnish
and brush
star stencil
masking tape
stencil brush
acrylic frosting
varnish

1 Sand the window frame then apply pale blue-green vinyl silk paint and leave to dry. For the glaze, mix one part deep blue-green emulsion (latex) to six parts scumble and apply. Draw the heart grainer "rocker" across the glazed surface and leave to dry, then varnish the whole frame.

2 Make sure that the glass is clean, and then attach the stencil with masking tape. Using a stencil brush, apply the frosting evenly through the stencil. Remove the stencil before the varnish dries completely.

green

Nature's colour of growth and hope, green is one of the primary colours of light. Historically, green pigment has come from the mineral malachite, from verdigris (the patina on the surface of copper) and even from highly toxic arsenic. Green is said to assist relaxation, concentration and meditation, all of which require a focused state of mind. The Georgians used a lot of pea green next to off-white, while Victorians preferred the more sombre olive green. Until fairly recently green was used on walls in only a pale, tinted form, but in the last decade or so ethnic influences have encouraged bolder attitudes towards home colour, and we can now buy green in wonderfully vibrant shades of lime, viridian, grass and emerald.

"nature's colour of growth,
hope and regeneration"

green palette

A glance across open countryside or even around a garden will reveal the incredible variety that exists in shades of green. A mixture of equal quantities of pure blue and yellow produces a bright grassy green, but as more yellow is added the colour turns to spring green, vibrant lime and eventually cool lemon. When more blue is added we get pine, sea green and viridian. Each of these shades can be varied by using a mixture of more specific or subtle blues and yellows.

BELOW Bottle Green provides an elegant look for a modern topiary.

BELOW Grass Green carries feelings of straightfoward happiness.

BELOW An Olive Green wreath is a sophisticated choice.

ABOVE Sea Green hearts look cool and inviting against chalk blue.

BELOW A white backdrop captures the richness of Leaf Green.

ABOVE Lime Green has a bold, fresh and ultimately irresistible look.

BELOW Moss Green describes the texture as much as the colour.

ABOVE Lemon Green creates a light, airy and fresh ambience.

BELOW Lichen Green is a soft, natural yellow-green.

bottle green

A deep, dark and dramatic colour, bottle green can look almost black in a dimly lit room. For this reason, good lighting is most important if you are considering using it as a wall colour. This is the colour of medieval velvet robes, wine bottles and ivy creeping across a brick wall. Bottle green looks smart with cream, and the two fade elegantly alongside each other. White is not so forgiving, however, and needs to be kept pristine to maintain the sharp, fresh contrast. For a brighter look, combine bottle green with earthy rusts or peachy orange.

rich, **opulent** shades of **bottle** green

RIGHT A glass bottle and lampshade show the many different shades of bottle green revealed by the addition of light.

OPPOSITE ABOVE Creamy whites combine with light bottle greens to create the freshest of displays.

OPPOSITE BELOW This decorative plait has a traditional country look.

grass green

You would have to live in a desert not to recognize grass green, which is, literally, the colour of a freshly mown summer lawn. It carries with it feelings of optimism, confidence and happiness, which makes it a good colour choice for children's rooms. This shade of green is often used for garden or conservatory furniture, perhaps because it looks so good in natural light and surrounded by other shades of green. Green has been called an "appetite colour" because it can trigger thoughts of food. This is why it is a popular choice in restaurants and is ideal for dining areas in the home. Team it with buttercup yellow and white for a fresh, summer-meadow effect or with sky blue and waxed bare wood to give a relaxed country feel.

OPPOSITE LEFT A flat green wall is the perfect backdrop for this very pretty pale grey marble table, which has been set with lemon green china and delicate glass-beaded candlesticks.

OPPOSITE RIGHT Green provides just the right feelings of freshness, youthfulness and fun in a family kitchen.

THIS PAGE The addition of a plain beaded throw gives this grass green room a relaxed, country feel.

citrus fruit bowl

You Will Need
soft pencil
tracing paper
stencil card (cardboard)
craft knife or scalpel
cutting mat
plain fruit bowl
cleaning fluid
cloth
masking tape
yellow chinagraph pencil
water-based ceramic
paint: citrus green,
mid-green, dark green
and yellow
artist's paintbrushes
paint palette
acrylic varnish (optional)

The combination of citrus yellow and green give a fresh, new look to a plain, china bowl. The limes are painted in an energetic freehand style and look terrific adorning this fruit bowl, making this the liveliest centrepiece ever to grace your table.

1 Draw a freehand lime on to tracing paper and transfer it to stencil card (cardboard). Cut out the lime stencil using a sharp craft knife or scalpel and a cutting mat.

3 Add mid-green highlights to the fruits and allow the paint to dry. Paint a stalk at the end of each lime in dark green. Let the paint dry.

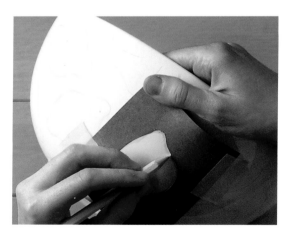

2 Attach the stencil to the bowl with masking tape. Draw inside the stencil on to the bowl using a yellow chinagraph pencil. Repeat to draw several limes all over the bowl. Fill the limes with citrus paint.

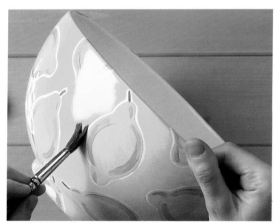

4 Paint the background yellow, leaving a thin white outline around each lime. Paint on varnish or bake the bowl in the oven according to the paint manufacturer's instructions.

olive green

The colour is described perfectly by its name, which immediately summons up mental images of bowls filled with glossy green olives. Olive green is a useful and versatile colour, and it adapts easily to any mood you wish to create. Used with gold, for instance, it proclaims opulence and grandeur, but alongside golden-yellow it has its roots firmly in the rainforest. In the wrong surroundings it can fade into the background and look rather dull, but it can also be a stylish choice for a sophisticated modern room.

Both the Arts and Crafts and the art nouveau movements favoured olive green in their designs, and it was seen again in the 1970s Victorian revival. These days olive green is popular once again, but is more likely to appear as a foil for brighter colours in ethnic-style decor.

ABOVE **Texture** has a major effect on olive green, as can be seen in the way the glossy glaze on this earthenware storage jar illuminates the colour.

OPPOSITE Olive green is a good colour for floors, and the stencilled pattern used here is practical, yet pretty enough to banish any military associations.

bowls filled with **glossy** green **olives**

sea green

The name encompasses a range of colours as wide as the ocean, from the bright blue-green of shallow water on the shoreline of the Mediterranean to the pale watery green of the ice-bound Arctic. Sea green is easy on the eye and is infinitely adaptable, looking cool or warm depending on the rest of the colour scheme. It is a colour that looks good outdoors in bright light where it actually improves as it fades.

distressed wall

You Will Need
light, medium and
dark shades of soft
green and white
silk-finish emulsion
(satin finish latex)
paint (buy a dark
shade and mix it
with white to make
the light and
medium shades)
large and medium
decorator's
paintbrushes
medium shade of
soft green matt
emulsion (flat latex)
paint
tissue paper
acrylic scumble
stippling brush
clean cotton rag

Frottage is an unusual and effective way to achieve a change of texture on a wall. It is not difficult to do and looks good on a wall divided by a dado (chair) rail. The colour and texture of the finished wall give an impression of verdigris, a naturally occurring patina on weathered copper.

1 Paint the upper part of the wall with two coats of light green silk-finish paint, leaving each to dry. Dilute the matt (flat) green paint with about 20% water. Brush this on to a section of the wall.

2 Immediately press a sheet of tissue paper over the entire surface except for a narrow band adjacent to the next section you will be working on. Work on a manageable area at a time.

3 Carefully peel back the tissue paper to reveal most of the base colour. Brush on two coats of medium green silk-finish paint over the textured wallpaper below the dado (chair) rail, leaving each to dry. If the wallpaper is new, it may bubble, but it will shrink back when dry.

4 Mix dark green silk finish with acrylic scumble in a ratio of one part paint to six parts scumble. Brush this glaze on to a section of the wallpaper.

5 Immediately dab over the wet glaze with a stippling brush to eliminate brushmarks and even out the texture.

6 Wipe a cotton cloth gently over the stippled glaze to remove it from the raised area of the wallpaper. Complete the wall section by section. Paint the dado rail with white paint, leave to dry and brush on the green glaze.

lime green

Bright, acid lime green on walls
is part of the colour revival that has been
inspired and encouraged by the current
media fascination with interior decorating.
Empowered by television and magazines,
people have been released from convention
and given the confidence to choose brighter,
bolder colours to make a statement – and
lime green certainly does that!

Lime green is cool – in every sense of the
word – and can be reinforced with other bold
colour choices, such as cobalt blue, chocolate
brown, burnt orange, shocking pink, deep
purple, gold and aluminium. If you like the
colour but don't want it to dominate, paint the
walls white and add accents of lime and other
hot colours with the soft furnishings. Smart
fittings such as aluminium rails keep the look
sharp and fresh.

invigorate
your home with **zesty** lime

OPPOSITE Lime green walls
and brilliant orange
crockery bring instant
sunshine to a kitchen.

ABOVE A mellower shade
of lime green is used with
a chic blend of natural
materials.

lemon green

Lemon green, a paler, less intense version of lime, has a name that conjures up the new, unripe fruit, and its delicacy is best captured when it is used in a translucent form. A good wall effect can be achieved by painting a basecoat of yellow then brushing over a tinted blue-green glaze. This will keep the colour light and add to its reflective quality.

Voile or muslin drapes in lemon green will cool a room without blocking all traces of the sunshine outside, and they are the perfect complement to each other, like a pitcher of lemonade and a sunny afternoon.

BELOW Lemon green gives a fresh and inviting look to walls.

OPPOSITE In warm, clever lighting, lemon green walls create a summery ambience.

leaf green

Leaf green is a colour that originates in nature. Individual associations vary according to the climate, but this is usually the green of perfect, mature leaves before they fade or take on their autumnal tints. A glance at a garden will show nature's variety, but, as a paint colour, a convincingly natural leaf green has always been quite difficult to mix. Dilution with white tends to flatten the colour and rob it of its life, but clever mixing or the use of a glaze over a flat colour will go some way towards capturing its luminosity. Go the whole way and use leaf green with other shades seen in nature – earthy brown, bleached wood and rust or other deeper greens. Pale creamy yellow or icy pale blue are good background colours, and red ochre, its complementary, provides the strongest contrast.

ABOVE A garden chair gets a witty interpretation with textured turf and cheerful daises.

LEFT The pattern on these vivid green curtains perfectly echoes the leaves of the plant, giving a summery feel.

place mat

These stylish place mats are very easy to make and add a contemporary look to the dinner table. The smaller, gently curving flower shape could be used to make coasters with napkins tied in co-ordinating colours.

You Will Need
tracing paper
pencil
medium weight
manilla card in two

colours
craft knife
cutting mat
high tack glue
flat cord

1 Make a template for the place mat then draw around the template on to the manilla cardboard. Make a pattern in the same way for the smaller inside shape and draw it on to the other colour of the card. Cut out both shapes using a craft knife and a cutting mat.

2 Draw the curved border line on to the base card in pencil. Apply a fine line of glue, following the drawn line, then carefully stick the flat cord over the glue line. Cut and butt up the cord ends where they meet. Glue the inside shape in place within the curved border.

the natural touch

Be inspired by the natural world and create a fresh look that is wholly up to date. The key to success lies in the plants, colours and materials you choose. Houseplants pass in and out of fashion: an aspidistra is definitely Victorian, cheese and spider plants were popular in the 1970s, and the current preference is for sculptural plants, such as clipped topiary or large succulents, to go with the modern look.

Textures of natural materials, such as rope, cane, hessian (burlap), wood, slate and leather, blend harmoniously, and their natural colouring needs little more than the right plants, a wooden floor and a pale, warm colour on the walls.

moss green

Moss is nature's soft green velvet carpet for woodland floors, and the name describes the texture as much as it does the colour. Moss green has freshness without fragility and looks good in large rooms with high ceilings or on sweeping staircases. It is a popular colour for carpets and sumptuous fabrics, such as velvets and silks, which drape well and catch the light.

key ring

This generously sized tassel, with its skirt of green garden twine, makes an impressive key ring. Worked over a curtain pole finial, the tassel uses the simplest of techniques to stunning effect. The striped cord is made using two different colours of twine.

You Will Need
twine in 2 colours
scissors
cup hook
hand drill
clamp (optional)
drill with wood bit
curtain pole finial
thick knitting needle
instant bonding glue
glue spreader
mounting board or
wood, 20 x 28cm/
8 x 11in

1 Cut both colours of twine into equal lengths and knot together. Secure the cup hook into the chuck of a hand drill and loop the twine through at one end, securing it over a door handle or clamp at the other. Turn the drill until the twine is tightly spun. Release the clamped end and attach to the cup hook, twisting to make a tight cord.

2 Drill a hole in the finial from top to bottom, glue the outside and wind the brown twine around it. Rotate the finial on a knitting needle to avoid overhandling. Cut even lengths of green twine and tie in the middle with twine. This can then be tied to the cord.

3 Liberally apply glue to the top of the skirt and thread the cord through the hole in the finial. Pull so the top of the skirt sits inside the finial. Trim the tassel to an even length.

lichen green

Lichen describes a soft, silvery green with a yellow cast. It takes its name from a strange compound of fungus and algae that appears on stones, walls and trees. It is a beautiful, soft, muted colour, which can match many different moods. The silver within it is cool and hard, its green element provides softness, and the yellow gives it warmth and life. These characteristics can either be brought into focus or subdued by your choice of surrounding colours and style of accessories.

An ideal colour for subdued northern light, lichen green is perfect for a Scandinavian-style room.

THIS PAGE Crushed velvet ribbons in lichen green add a touch of luxury to a plain bed throw. The colour is also picked up, in a slightly darker shade, in the cushion.

OPPOSITE The pale lichen green wall colour looks mellow and tranquil in the subdued natural sunlight.

white

Purists may argue that white is not a colour, but it is recognized and described as one by all who use it. Leonardo da Vinci proclaimed white to be the "first of all simple colours", and we associate it with cleanliness, purity and light. White is the lightest, most reflective and expansive of all colours and is associated with chastity and innocence. It illuminates other colours and brings them to life without detracting from or influencing them in any other way. There are thousands of variations of white, and the human eye is adept at recognizing many of them. Choosing white for your walls is not as easy as it used to be as the range of whites available to the decorator grows wider all the time.

"we associate white with cleanliness, purity, innocence and light"

white palette

Just as a heavy snowfall redefines a familiar landscape, a coat of white paint appears to change the proportions of a room. White can be used to highlight architectural features, such as plaster mouldings, when set against another colour, or it can just as easily hide unwanted features. If everything is painted white you get a "blank canvas" effect.

Black and white create the strongest light–dark contrast, but the effect can be too stark and require the addition of other colours for life and warmth.

BELOW **Snow White gives a dazzling fresh, crisp white.**

BELOW **Ivory Lace diffuses the sunlight in this beautiful curtain.**

BELOW **China tableware in Butter Cream provides an elegant touch.**

ABOVE **Black and White create a sophisticated contrast.**

ABOVE **Clear glass, like water, reflects light as white.**

ABOVE **Silver and white create a cool, contemporary look.**

BELOW **Decorated natural fabric makes an interesting wall hanging.**

BELOW **Shells and stones give this box a sculptural elegance.**

BELOW **Wooden lime-washed floors make a room seem more spacious.**

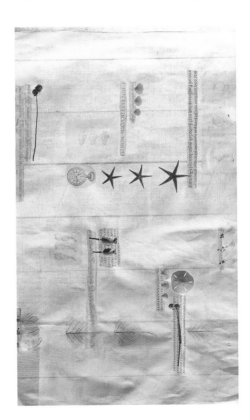

snow white

This is the most reflective of all whites, capable of dazzling and disturbing the eyes. It is also the most popular, versatile, useful and least expensive paint on the market. This is the paint to reach for when you move into a new house or apartment and want to start afresh by eliminating every trace of the previous occupant's decorating disasters. It will allow you to see the proportions and make decorating decisions with clarity.

   You may love your white walls and never want to change them, but if you do choose to apply colour, snow white is the ideal undercoat because it reflects the top coat's colour back at itself to give it maximum intensity.

OPPOSITE White walls, soft voile bedding and natural wood give this room a sense of elegant tranquillity.

THIS PAGE Chalky walls, starched cotton and shiny china surround this wonderful flower arrangement.

ivory lace

Ivory is a mellow white, easier on the eyes and more flattering to the complexion than bright white. Natural ivory yellows with age, and the name is applied across a range of warm, pale shades of white. Perhaps our most familiar visual reference for the colour would be a piano, where black ebony and white ivory make up the keys. The combination can be used to dramatic effect when decorating, and a black and ivory white checkerboard floor, immortalized in the paintings of Dutch interiors, has remained popular for hundreds of years.

Ivory walls, carpeting and soft furnishings are totally impractical in rooms used by young children, so the choice is both sophisticated and extravagant. This has made ivory a favourite with upmarket interior designers, who mix it with natural materials and fabrics, such as muslin, linen, leather, bleached and waxed wood, stone and rope.

While bright white suits bright sunshine, it looks chilly in a cloudy climate, but ivory reflects any incoming light and instils warmth. Use it with muted dark colours, such as Prussian blue.

OPPOSITE **The classic shape and colour of this vase make it the perfect receptacle for an elegant arrangement of ivory-coloured tulips.**

ABOVE **Fluted corrugated cardboard and woven ivory-coloured fabric have been combined to make an extremely stylish lamp.**

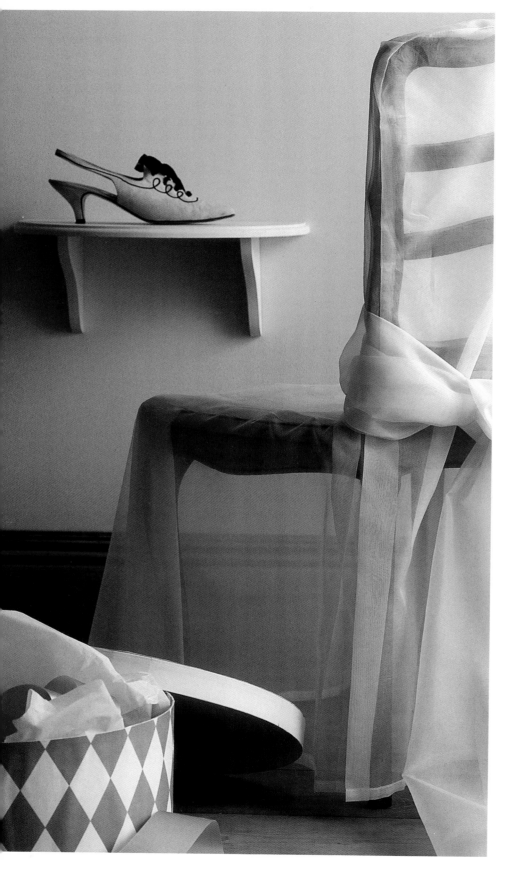

butter cream

This rich, yellowy cream was the most popular colour for interior woodwork during the Edwardian period, when light colours and pretty patterns replaced the gloom of the late Victorian years. Now, however, it is most often used as part of the country-decorating palette, in which Shaker style and historic colours combine in harmonious simplicity.

Butter cream looks good in a gloss finish, making window frames and other woodwork look simply delicious. Used in this way, it looks surprisingly good with matt white walls and also combines well with most other colours. In modern living rooms and entrance halls it is a useful way to take the cold edge off minimalist styling.

LEFT **Walls clad in butter cream add a warm nostalgic feel to an interior, here enchanced by the choice of accessories.**

bucket stool

Florist's buckets in galvanized tin are widely available in a variety of heights, and for this project the taller the bucket, the better. For a touch of milking parlour nostalgia choose a cream waffle tea towel (dish cloth) for the seat.

You Will Need

1m/1yd heavy cord or rope
2 florist's buckets
glue gun
large self-cover buttons
material scraps for buttons

fabric cutting tool for buttons
waffle tea towel (dish cloth)
circular cushion pad
large sewing needle
matching thread

Attach the cord or rope to the top rim of one of the buckets using the glue gun. Place this bucket inside the second bucket, applying glue to its rim, then invert both buckets. Use the fabric to cover the buttons.

Sew the buttons through the waffle hand towel. Use the towel to cover the cushion pad. Instead of smoothing out the gathering in the fabric, accentuate it, using the buttons as a focus. Glue the pad to the bucket.

cream

Cream is a neutral white with a slightly yellow cast and no trace of grey or pink, unlike the ubiquitous magnolia. Older properties will always look better painted cream than stark white because bright titanium white was a 20th-century invention, and the white pigments used before it was available yellowed naturally with age. It is a classically elegant colour. In a modern setting, cream will have a warming effect on even stark, minimalist interiors, and it is an integral part of the "new" natural colour scheme, where it mixes well with pale slate grey, stone, suede and chocolate browns. Cream is an ideal choice for this style, with its emphasis on space, light, comfort, natural materials and interesting shapes.

black and white

The extremes of contrast in dark and light, black and white carry so many universally recognized associations, from chessboards and zebra skins to piano keys. Cole Porter wrote a marvellous song about a famous decorator called Elsie de Wolfe (later Lady Mendl), whose black-and-white style had a huge influence on decorating in the 1920s.

The starkness of the black–white contrast lacks warmth and is more likely to be seen in stylish galleries and offices than in a family home. To introduce warmth without adding other colours, choose polished wooden floors, textured fabrics, plants and warm lighting.

chessboards to taxicabs, zebra skins to **piano keys**

OPPOSITE ABOVE **Fabric, draped in the Regency style, makes an elegant, sophisticated window treatment.**

OPPOSITE BELOW **A perfect balance of contrasts here with black and white: soft and textured.**

LEFT **An unusual arrangement of floor tiles creates large black crosses.**

Japanese screen

You Will Need
garden trellis
blackboard paint
paintbrush
heavyweight tracing
paper
staple gun
craft knife
red emulsion
(latex) paint
drill
2 screw eyes
tape measure
wire coat hanger
pliers
2 picture hooks

A black-and-white window screen with a few well-chosen pieces of furniture gives this room an almost authentic Japanese look. The wooden screen is actually a simple garden trellis, painted black and backed with semi-transparent draughtsman's tracing paper. The walls and woodwork have been painted the same creamy white colour. This screen is the perfect treatment for a minimalist room.

Paint the trellis black, and leave to dry. Paint one square red for added interest. Blackboard paint creates a perfectly matt finish, but other matt or gloss paints can be used. Staple sheets of tracing paper to the back of the trellis, and trim to ensure there are no overlaps.

Drill a very fine hole in the top of the trellis at the end of the first strut in from each end. Screw a screw eye into each hole.

Measure the length of the window to determine how long the hooks for hanging should be. The base of the screen should touch the window frame below. Cut two pieces of coat hanger wire to the correct length for the hooks. Then hang the screen on these from picture hooks.

translucence

The effect of light passing through an imperfectly clear material, such as frosted glass or sheer white voile, produces an effect we call translucence. This is not a pigment, but is the way we perceive and illustrate light. Translucence produces a softening of hard edges and a very gentle, flattering light.

This quality of translucence is best revealed when glass, or another transparent material, is surrounded by a more solid version of white or another very pale colour, so that light creates soft reflections on its surface. Muslin-shaded windows, misty window panes, floating candles in a glass bowl or a milky glaze on a wall all produce a translucent effect.

OPPOSITE Soft lighting on glass, polished silver, white muslin and petals creates a pretty, translucent effect.

ABOVE The effect of the lighted candle and floating petals is enhanced by reflections in the water and on the glass.

molten silver

The industrial pressed steel look came in with high tech and the New York loft style and has refused to go away. It may have had its roots in industry, but molten silver is now one of the most popular looks for the home. Metallic finishes no longer have to be cold and hard, because you can buy convincing acrylic paints in most metal shades, and these are suitable for painting on any surface. Dull molten silver is cool in both senses of the word and can take the excitement of being mixed with vibrant colours. Go for the retro look with American diner styling or stay aloof with black, white and grey.

THIS PAGE Silver combined with white light creates a warming effect.

OPPOSITE The shine turns grey into silver. Shot silk is dressed up with a latticework of silver trimmings.

natural fabric

These might be called feel-good fabrics – the linens, raffias, hemps and muslins whose irregularities we cherish because they are the very antithesis of man-made uniformity. The colours come from plants and from fibres ripened and bleached by the sun.

The natural look has come of age with the millennium, as people everywhere become aware of the need to value the planet's limited resources. Use stone, wood, glass, baskets and plants, and neutral, light-enhancing colours to create a naturally mellow environment.

BELOW Sweet dreams are guaranteed in the restful natural shades of the fresh linen sheets and a headboard softened by coils of soft rope.

ABOVE LEFT Each curtain tab is decorated with a woven hemp ribbon and a different dried, scented spice pod.

ABOVE RIGHT Cross-sections of the natural world are framed and celebrated in a beautiful hessian (burlap) curtain.

LEFT These loosely woven brown linen curtains reflect the essence of modern, naturally elegant style.

BELOW Golden light filtering through a woven raffia blind brings a nostalgic Robinson Crusoe look to any room.

7

In recent years, our need to feel in touch with nature and concerns for the environment have led to a revival of interest in natural materials. Shells and Stones are perhaps an unusual decorative material for the home, but in a simple interior can breathe life into a room. Make the most of *objets trouvés* brought back as souvenirs from trips to the seaside – collecting shells and pebbles at the beach is even more addictive if you know you are going to use them later.

shells & stones

ABOVE LEFT Bring a touch of class and a quirky seaside style to a simple brown paper lampshade. Using pebbles worn smooth by sea-waters and picked up at the beach, you can create a work of art that is truly individual.

LEFT Pebbles, cobbles and stone have been used the world over to create beautifully classic yet hardwearing floors. The simple checkerboard design here looks stunning in its simplicity.

delight in the beauty and coolness of
sea-washed pebbles

shell curtain

If you love to be beside the seaside, this is the perfect way to express that feeling. It is simple enough to make in an afternoon with a pocketful of shells, and some fine cotton sheeting.

The elegance of this curtain is easy to achieve by drilling shells and stitching them onto a curtain. Once made, simply peg it up on a piece of string with clothes pegs.

You Will Need
tape measure
lightweight cotton,
polycotton or
muslin fabric
scissors
needle
thread
mini drill
assorted small shells
reusable tacky putty
cord
wooden clothes pegs
screw eyes

1 Measure your window and cut enough fabric to cover it, allowing extra for a slight gather and seams and hems. Make up the curtain.

2 Drill a hole in each of the shells and then stitch the shells onto the curtain in staggered rows, approximately 7.5cm/3in apart.

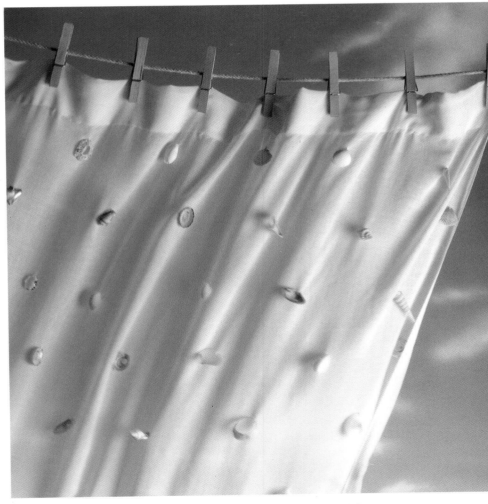

3 Thread the cord through the holes in the wooden clothes pegs: the larger the hole, the more easily the curtain will draw back. Attach the cord to your window frame using screw eyes. Clip the pegs to the top of the curtain.

wood

A wood-brown and white combination is delicious. Natural wood shades range from yellow through red to deep grey-brown, and applications of wax polish or varnish will preserve and enrich the surface of any type of wood. Because wood has always been a building material, it is impossible to imagine it looking out of place in our homes. People have a natural affinity for wood.

breathe new life into your **home** with the simple **elegance** of natural wood

As a rule, golden wood shades suit bold bright colours, while limed and bleached woods look best with pale colours. Dark woods suit cream or ethnic-style fabrics.

OPPOSITE **The simple elegance of the pure white drapes provides a perfect background for an antique wooden folding chair.**

ABOVE RIGHT **Natural textures are provided by twisted willow, a brown glazed pot, a thick twist of rope and a woven cane chest.**

BELOW RIGHT **The woven twig-work and crisply starched cotton bed linen make an interesting contrast of rough brown and smooth white.**

natural tones

The palette of natural tones represents the recent fusion between fashion and interior design. The cool, expensive, elegant style appeared first on the catwalk, but the style was soon adopted for interiors, initially in design studios and shops but then in domestic settings. After all, the clothes look best in an appropriately stylish environment.

Natural fabrics, mixed with bare wood, glass, metal and earthenware, and the non-colours, in shades such as taupe, khaki, grey, oatmeal and white, declare allegiance to this sophisticated, uncluttered style.

stockists

Atlantis Art Materials

146 Brick Lane

London EC1 6RU

Corres Mexican Tiles Ltd

Unit 1A Station Road

Hampton Wick

Kingston

Surrey KT1 4HG

Tel: 0181 943 4142

Crown Paints

Crown Decorative

Products Ltd

P.O. Box 37

Crown House

Hollins Road

Darwen

Lancashire BB3 0BG

Ellis and Farrier

20 Beak Street

London

W1R 3HA

BEADS, SEQUINS

E. Ploton Ltd

273 Archway Road

London

N6 5AA

ART AND GILDING

MATERIALS

Europacrafts

Hawthorn Avenue

Hull

HU3 5JZ

Tel: 01482 223 399

John Lewis Plc

Oxford Street

London

W1A 1EX

(Branches throughout the

country)

FABRICS, FURNISHING

FABRICS, TRIMMINGS,

RIBBONS, BEADS,

CURTAIN TAPES

Mosaic Workshop

1a Princeton Street

London

WC1R 4AX

Tel: 0171 404 9249

Nuline

315 Westbourne Park Road

London W11

GENERAL HARDWARE,

SHEET METAL SUPPLIERS

Paint Magic

79 Shepperton Road

Islington

London N1 3DF

Panduro Hobby

Westward House

Transport Avenue

Brentford

Middlesex

TW8 9HF

Woolfin Textiles & Co

64 Great Titchfield

Street

London W1

RANGE OF NATURAL

FABRICS,

CALICO,

HESSIAN (BURLAP)

Worlds End Tiles

Silverthorne Road

Battersea

London

SW8 3HE

Tel: 0171 720 8358

RANGE OF TILES

UNITED STATES

Art Essentials of New York Ltd

3 Cross Street

Suffern

NY

10901

Tel: (800) 283 5323

Brian's Crafts Unlimited

P.O. Box 731046

Ormond Beach

FL 32173-046

Tel: (904) 672 2726

Britex Fabrics

146 Geary Street

San Francisco

CA 94108

FABRICS, WIDE

RANGE OF GENERAL

CRAFT MATERIALS

AND EQUIPMENT

Createx Colors

14 Airport Park Road

East Granby

CT

06026

Tel: (860) 653 5505

Dick Blick

P.O. Box 1267

Galesburg

IL 61402

Tel: (309) 343 6181

Eastern Art Glass

P.O. Box 341

Wyckoff

NJ 07481

Tel: (201) 847 0001

Hofcraft

P.O. Box 72

Grand Haven

MI 49417

Tel: (800) 828 0359

Ideal Tile of

Manhattan. Inc

405 East 51st St

Peekskill

NY 10022

Tel: (212) 759 2339

Peal Paint

Canal Street

NY 10011

The Art Store

935 Erie Blvd. E.

Syracuse,

NY 13210

CANADA

Abbey Arts & Crafts

4118 East Hastings Street

Vancouver BC

Tel: 299 5201

Lewiscraft

2300 Yonge Street

Toronto

Ontario M4P 1E4

AUSTRALIA

Camden Arts Centre

Pty Ltd

188-200 Gertrude Street

Fitzroy

Australia

3065

Hobby Co

402

Gallery Level

197 Pitt Street

Sydney

Australia

Tel: (02) 221 0666

Rodda Pty Ltd

62 Beach Street

Port Melbourne

Victoria

Australia

Spotlight (60 stores)

Tel: (freecall) 1800 500021

W M Crosbey

(Merchandise) Pty Ltd

266-274

King Street

Melbourne

Australia

3000